Guppies, Mollies, and Platys

Everything About Purch
Nutrition, and Behavior

Filled with Full-color Photographs

BARRON'S

Contents

Appropriate Accommodations

Overall Health Program

Appendix

Introduction

Introducing Four Families

Live-bearing fish have been a fixture in aquariums ever since the end of the nineteenth century. They contributed significantly to the surge in popularity of this hobby in the twentieth

> Many live-bearers come from small bodies of running water.

century. Many aquarists had their first aquarium experiences with these fish— as I did. It is pleasurable to watch these beautiful fish. They also offer the beginner the experience of following a live birth. Even professionals continue to discover fascinating things with these fish.

Classification and Origin

Live-bearing does not designate any systematic whole. This phenomenon is characteristic of several fish families. The species presented belong to four families:

> Live-bearing toothcarps, the Poeciliidae family: the approximately 260 species are native to the United States, the Caribbean Islands, and as far south as Argentina.

> Goodeids, the Goodeidae family: they come from only Mexico and in particular from the highlands. The approximately 35 species make up the second largest family of live-bearers.

> Live-bearing Halfbeaks, the Hemirhamphidae family: the approximately 35 species live in Southeast Asia.

> Four-eyed fish, the Anablepidae family: the approximately 15 species live in Central and South America.

Only a few live-bearers are available in the marketplace. Mostly they are the colorful breeding forms of Guppies, Platys, Mollies, and Swordtails.

TIP

Coming to Grips with the Results of Live Birth

The special feature of live birth has contributed to the popularity of the live-bearers. They produce young that are already miniature versions of their parents. Here is what to look for:

> The baby fish can immediately swim and eat. They can even take care of themselves, but you must feed the baby fish right away.

> Since the baby fish are relatively large, quite a number of them survive in the aquarium. So the question arises about what to do with them (See p. 40).

Lifestyle

The smaller live-bearers up to about 2 inches (5 cm) seek out shelter from plants and overhanging grasses at the edges of the waters in which they live. With the exception of the Halfbeaks, which swim in the upper reaches and even right under the surface of the water, the smaller species use all layers of the water.

Many larger species prefer open water, where they often live in small schools. Since the males of many species are quite aggressive toward one another (see "Live-bearer Portraits," pages 14–17), the schools often consist of just one male and numerous females.

Natural Enemies

Most live-bearers are small to medium in size. Thus they have many enemies—both in the water and in the air. But because they give birth to live, fully developed young, live-bearers have a better chance of survival than fish that have to develop from eggs.

Please be mindful of socialization inside the aquarium. Do not put live-bearers with

> *Colorful Guppies made the live-bearers popular.*

predators such as Angelfish if you expect the offspring to survive.

What Is Live Birth?

The young of live-bearers hatch out of the eggs inside the womb and are born live. During their development, the young get their nutrients from the yolk of the egg. With many species such as the Goodeids, they are nourished by the mother through a structure similar to an umbilical cord.

GOOD TO KNOW

Family Classifications

The species mentioned above belong to the following families:

✔ **The Poeciliidae family:**
Black Metallic Live-bearer
Humpbacked Limia
Guppy
Short-finned Molly
Sailfin Molly
Blue-eyed Toothcarp
Swordtail
Platy
Variegated Platy

✔ **The Goodeidae Family**
Red-tailed Goodeid

✔ **The Hemirhamphidae Family**
Wrestling Halfbeak
Celebes Halfbeak

7

Information on Breeding Forms

Guppies, Platys, Swordtails, and Mollies have been kept in aquariums for about a hundred years. In this time, many of the very beautiful breeding forms have been developed. They now make up the majority of the live-bearers that are available commercially.

> Double Swordtails are highly esteemed because of the beautiful shape of their fins.

A Little Anatomy

Like most fish, live-bearers have dorsal, tail, and anal fins plus two ventral and two pectoral fins. With nearly all species, the males are smaller and slimmer than the females. The latter sometimes become very fat. The sexes are particularly easy to distinguish in live-bearing tooth-carps because of the male's gonopodium (the anal fin that has evolved into a reproductive organ; see p. 41). Also, many females have a gravid spot (see photo, p. 40). With Goodeids and Halfbeaks, the anal fin is only partially transformed into a gonopodium. To recognize this, you have to look quite closely.

With many species, the scales are easy to see. With healthy fish, they should be complete and must lie flat (also see p. 35).

Many Colors

The wild forms of the Guppy have remarkably varied colors. No two males have precisely the same coloring. You will see this when your Guppies have babies. With Platys, Swordtails, and Mollies, breeders have crossed fish to produce variations mainly in colors and fins.

TIP

How to Find a Breeding Pair of Guppies

If you are looking for a breeding pair of Guppies of a specific kind, here are some helpful hints:

➤ Females from largefins (see p. 9) have a little less color in the tail fin than the males.

➤ Shortfin and swordfin females have colorless and shorter fins than the males.

➤ Blond Guppies are colored like albinos but have black eyes. So look at the eyes to make sure you have two of the same kind.

In addition, active breeding produces spontaneous changes in heredity (mutations), so some fish have colors and fin shapes that are different from those of their parents. As a result, a beautiful form of live-bearer could arise unexpectedly, even in your aquarium.

Selective Breeding of Guppies

In order to organize the breeding forms of Guppies, many years ago the International Selective Breeding Standard (ISBS) was developed. This describes the ideal size, markings, coloration, and fin shapes of the Guppies selected for breeding.

Tail Fins: There are twelve shapes distinguished in the ISBS in combination with an established dorsal fin shape (see illustrations pp. 9 and 10). Guppies are divided into three breed groups based on the shape of the tail fin:

➤ Largefin with veil-, delta-, fan-, and flagtail.

➤ Swordtails with top, bottom, and double sword as well as lyretail.

➤ Shortfins with round-, spade-, spear-, and needletail

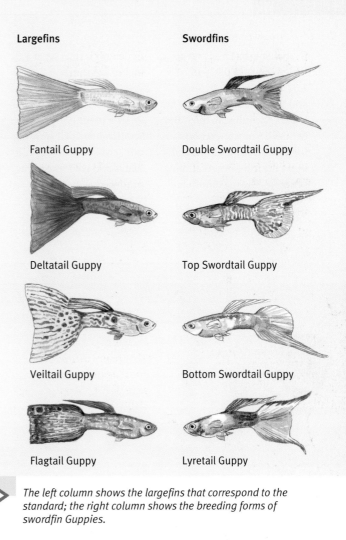

Largefins

Fantail Guppy

Deltatail Guppy

Veiltail Guppy

Flagtail Guppy

Swordfins

Double Swordtail Guppy

Top Swordtail Guppy

Bottom Swordtail Guppy

Lyretail Guppy

> *The left column shows the largefins that correspond to the standard; the right column shows the breeding forms of swordfin Guppies.*

Colors: Here, too, there are standards. They are distinguished according to background and cover colors. Both males and females exhibit the background colors, but the cover colors are exhibited almost exclusively by the more colorful males. Background colors include wild gray, blond, and blue.

Body Length: This is specified precisely at 0.936 to 1.01 inches (24 to 26 mm), and the same applies to the fin length. According to the ISBS, the tail fin must never be so long that it hangs down and keeps the fish from swimming properly. The maximum tail fin length is thus set at 1.01 inches (26 mm).

Selective Breeding with Platys

Shortly after their introduction, crosses between wild Platys and wild Swordfins produced characteristic red fish, the original form of all red breeding types of Platys and Swordtails.

Fin Shapes: As with Guppies, mutations produced fins with different shapes. There are, for example, the following:

➤ Simpson, also referred to as the Delta: a distinguishing feature is an enlarged dorsal fin.

➤ Brushtail (see photos, pages 3 and 26): the central rays of the tail fin are elongated.

➤ Lyre- or Dragontail: the first rays of the dorsal and the outer rays of the tail fin are attractively elongated. So-called Veiltails, in which all fins grow without limit, are poor swimmers and are undesirable for breeding.

Markings: In the wild, Platys exhibit distinguishing (usually black) spots on their body and especially in front of the tailfin, for which they are also bred selectively (see photo, p.24). This is how such fish as checkered Platys and Tuxedo Platys (with a wedge-shaped black spot on the side of their body) came to be. The Wagtail configuration is particularly well-known (see photos, pages 3 and 34); in this instance, all fin rays are black.

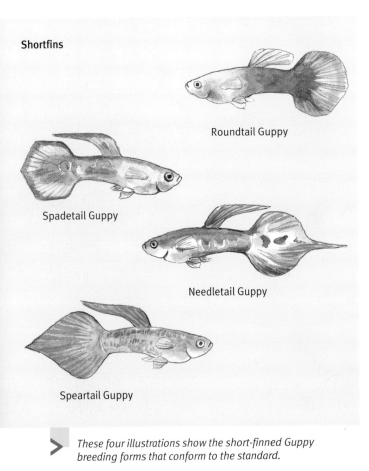

Shortfins

Roundtail Guppy

Spadetail Guppy

Needletail Guppy

Speartail Guppy

> These four illustrations show the short-finned Guppy breeding forms that conform to the standard.

> *The Speartail Guppy is a rare standard, and breeding it requires some knowledge of genetics.*

Selective Breeding of Swordtails

With Swordtails, there are the same breeding forms as with Platys. An important difference is the male's "sword," as the greatly elongated, colorful, lower tail fin ray is called. In wild types, the sword is yellow inside and black on the outside. However, breeding forms may exhibit the widest variety of colors. As for length, the standard prescribes half to two-thirds of the body length. Swordtails also resemble Platys in regard to fin shape. Fish with limitless fin growth are undesirable.

Swordtails grow to be much larger than Platys, though.

Handsome males can be over 3 inches (8 cm) long.

Selective Breeding of Mollies

With Mollies (see p. 19) there is one type with few dorsal fin rays that is derived from the Short-finned Molly (*Poecilia sphenops*; see portrait on p. 15) and its relatives. Another type has many dorsal fin rays and is descended from the Sailfin Molly (*Poecilia velifera*; see portrait on p. 15). The black breeding form, the Black Molly (see photo, p. 50), is particularly well-known as is the golden form, the Gold Molly (see photo, p. 18). Like all breeding forms, both of these were produced by crossing various Molly forms and types. In large- and lyrefin types, all fins are enlarged. In the Double swordtails, the upper and lower rays of the tail fin are greatly elongated.

TIP

Identifying Early- and Late-Maturing Males

➤ Early maturing males remain smaller and slimmer than normal males, and they produce fewer offspring. They are recognizable by the gonopodium (see p. 41), which develops when Platys reach a little more than 0.5 inches (1.5 cm) in length and when Molly and Swordtail males reach 1 inch (2.5 cm).

➤ Late-maturing males resemble the females for a long time. Many aquarists have become annoyed because instead of a female they ended up with a late-maturing male. At point of purchase, look for the gravid spot (see p. 40), which the males lack.

A Little Information About Heredity

The guppies in our aquarium, with their attractive markings and impressive fin shapes, are the product of either spontaneous mutations or selective breeding. I have no intention of motivating beginners to attempt breeding since it requires special

> The goal of breeding is male Guppies that look as much as possible like one another.

knowledge. Rather, I am much more interested in introducing them to the breeders' regular fare, for that will help them distinguish the various breeding forms more easily.

Breeding for Color

The basic color of all guppies in the wild is known as gray or wild gray. With breeding, though, there are always deviations in the coloring due to modifications in the genes. The wild-color trait always asserts itself, however. In the parlance of breeders, it is dominant. Conversely, the mutations in the wild color are overshadowed; they are recessive.

One of the most common mutations with guppies involves the suppression of black pigmentation, resulting in blond guppies. The body of blond female guppies is nearly flesh colored; with males there are only red and yellow hues. However, the eyes remain dark (in contrast to albinos, which have red eyes).

The wild-gray trait is dominant over the blond trait. However, if a blond guppy is crossed with a wild-colored one, all offspring are gray. These offspring carry hidden inside themselves the gene for blond coloration. If two of these fish are crossed with one another, 25 percent of the offspring consist of gray fish, which in turn always produce only gray offspring; 50 percent are gray on the outside but bear the gene for blond coloration; and 25 percent are blond Guppies. When these blond guppies are crossed with one another, all young are blonde.

Crossing Longfins

With long-finned live-bearing breeding forms, the males nearly always have an excessively long gonopodium (see p. 41), which is no longer useful in fertilizing the females. In order to produce live-bearers with long fins anyway, breeders make use of the dominance of the long fin trait. They cross a male with normal fins and a

> *A roundtail guppy with what is known as Moscow coloration. With this breeding form, the forward part of the body can become lighter or darker, depending on mood.*

long-finned, slightly dragon-finned female. Half of the offspring have long fins, and the other half have short ones. **Should longfins even be bred?** As you have already seen, the male longfins are not capable of fertilizing the females. The males, however, do not care that they cannot deliver their sperm. What matters to them is being able to perform their mating dance properly (see p. 40). Thus, breeders designate as undesirable only the fish that can no longer swim properly because of the length of their long fins and exclude them from further breeding.

Sperm Storage

Female live-bearing tooth-carps can store the male's sperm inside their body and use it to bear young several times in succession. This is known as sperm storage.

Even if you have bought only females, young fish in the broadest array of colors and fin shapes may suddenly appear in your aquarium. (See the tip on p. 40 for ideas on how to deal with this.) If you do not have any particular desires concerning the fry, you can simply enjoy the fantasy of nature. If you want to pass on the traits of a particularly handsome male, that also is no problem, for the old sperm is dislodged with every new fertilization. That is, after successful copulation, a female stores the sperm of the last "desirable" male.

13

Black Metallic Live-bearer
Girardinus metallicus

Humpback Limia
Limia nigrofasciata

Guppy
Poecilia reticulata

Characteristics: The males reach a length of about 1.5 inches (4 cm), the females 2.75 inches (7 cm). Even at an early age, the males are distinguished from the females by their black belly.
Distribution: Cuba.
Living Conditions: Aquarium of at least 15 gallons (57 L). Hard water, 73–79°F (23–26°C). Easy to care for. Plenty of plants. Very peaceable species.
Feeding: Omnivore, both dry and frozen food.
Reproduction: During the courtship display, the males swim in front of the females, then slowly float over them, and mate from the rear. The young, up to 50 in number, are born at intervals of about four weeks to several months. They grow slowly. They take at least six months to reach adulthood.

Characteristics: Males and females reach a length of 2.75 inches (7 cm). Males over a year old develop a hump—hence the name.
Distribution: Haiti. The native water is Miragoane Lake.
Living Conditions: Aquarium of at least 25 gallons (76 L). Hard water, 77–82°F (25–28°C). Humpbacks need lots of fresh water and frequent partial water changes. Lots of plants. Peaceable species.
Feeding: Omnivore, both dry and frozen food.
Reproduction: Up to 30 young are born at intervals of about four weeks.
Special Note: The sexes are easy to distinguish by the male's gonopodium (see p. 41). This species includes early-maturing males (see p. 11).

Characteristics: The multi-colored wild guppy males reach a length of 1 inch (2.5 cm); the colorless females reach 2 inches (5 cm).
Distribution: Originally northern South America, subsequently transplanted worldwide for mosquito control. Also found in brackish water.
Living Conditions: Aquarium of at least 15 gallons (57 L). Hard to soft water, 72–82°F (22–28°C). Easy to care for. Provide hiding places among plants. Very peaceable species.
Feeding: Omnivore.
Reproduction: In the demanding courtship display, the male dances around the female. Produce up to 100 young.
Special Note: The sexes are easy to distinguish by the male's gonopodium (see p. 41) and the female's gravid spot (see photo, p. 40).

 Aquarium of at least 15 gallons (57 L)

Aquarium of at least 20 gallons (80 L)

Aquarium of at least 45 gallons (170 L)

Short-finned Molly
Poecilia sphenops

Sailfin Molly
Poecilia velifera

Blue-eye Toothcarp
Priapella intermedia

Characteristics: Males and females reach a length of up to 2.75 inches (7 cm). The dorsal fins have only a few rays. The body is a shimmering bluish color with red dots. The fins are generally red.
Distribution: Central America, Mexico, and Guatemala.
Living Conditions: Aquarium of at least 22 gallons (76 L). Medium hard to hard water, 72–82°F (22–28°C). Frequent water changes. Lots of plants. Males are aggressive toward one another.
Feeding: Algae eater.
Reproduction: In the courtship display, the male pursues the female extensively. About every four weeks, the females give birth to up to 40 young that are already quite large.
Special Note: These Mollies may include some early-maturing males (see p. 11).

Characteristics: Males reach a length of up to 4 inches (10 cm), females up to 4.75 inches (12 cm). Males have sail-like dorsal fins.
Distribution: Mexico, Yucatan Peninsula. Also brackish water.
Living Conditions: Aquarium of at least 45 gallons (170 L). Very hard water, 75–86°F (24–30°C). Easy to care for. Males aggressive toward one another.
Feeding: Algae eaters that need lots of green food.
Reproduction: In the courtship display the males keep their dorsal fins stiff and dance in front of the females. Every four to six weeks, the females can produce 100 young.
Special Note: At an early age, males can be recognized by their gonopodium. They develop large dorsal fins only in large aquariums.

Characteristics: Males are fully grown at 2.5 inches (6 cm); females grow a little larger. The blue eyes on a yellow background are visible early.
Distribution: Mexico, in the vicinity of Palenque.
Living Conditions: Aquariums of at least 29 gallons (110 L). Hard water, 72–75°F (22–24°C). Strong current and frequent water changes. Lots of plants in only the back-ground to preserve lots of swimming room in the fore-ground. Peaceable species. Keep only in groups.
Feeding: Lots of live or frozen food but also likes small flies.
Reproduction: Inconspicuous courtship display. Up to 25 young born every four weeks.
Special Note: The only way to distinguish males from females is through the gonopodium (see p. 41).

Green Swordtail
Xiphophorus hellerii

Platy
Xiphophorus maculatus

Variegated Platy
Xiphophorus variatus

Characteristics: Not counting tail, males reach 3 inches (8 cm), females up to 4 inches (10 cm).
Distribution: Northern Central America.
Living Conditions: Aquariums of at least 45 gallons (170 L), for the fish are active swimmers. Hard water, 72–82°F (22–28°C). Mild current and regular water changes. Plants in only the background. Males are aggressive toward one another; keep one male with three to five females. Peaceable with other fish.
Feeding: Omnivore.
Reproduction: Attractive courtship display (crescent dance) by the male. Approximately every four weeks the females produce up to 100 young (large females can produce 200).
Special Note: Early-maturing males are common (see p. 11).

Characteristics: Males are full-grown at 1.75 inches (4.5 cm), females at 2.5 inches (6 cm).
Distribution: From Mexico to Honduras border.
Living Conditions: Aquarium of at least 15 gallons (57 L). Hard water, 71–82°F (20–28°C). Mild current. Change water every two weeks. Lots of vegetation required. Peaceable species; gets along well with many other types of fish.
Feeding: Much variety with dry and frozen food.
Reproduction: Inconspicuous courtship display. Females produce up to 100 young, but usually significantly fewer, about every four weeks.
Special Note: The male's gonopodium becomes visible early in life (see p. 41). Early-maturing males (see p. 11) occur starting at a length of about 0.5 inch (1 cm).

Characteristics: Males and females reach a length of about 2.5 inches (6 cm). They are distinguished from Platys (see center column) by a noticeably more slender body.
Distribution: Highlands around Mexico City and southward.
Living Conditions: Aquarium of at least 15 gallons (57 L). Hard water, 65–75°F (18–24°C); species can thus be kept in unheated indoor aquariums. Frequent water change required. Peaceable species.
Feeding: Plenty of variety with dry and frozen food.
Reproduction: The males spread their fins and display in front of the females. The females give birth to up to 40 young; they grow slowly and take a year to reach adulthood.

 Aquarium of at least 15 gallons (57 L)

Aquarium of at least 20 gallons (76 L)

 Aquarium of at least 45 gallons (170 L)

Redtail Splitfin or Redtail Goodeid
Xenotoca eiseni

Characteristics: Males grow to a length of nearly 2.5 inches (6 cm), females to 2.75 inches (7 cm). As they age, their back profile rises.
Distribution: Highlands of Mexico.
Living Conditions: Aquarium of at least 20 gallons (76 L). Hard water, 64–75°F (18–24°C). Easy to care for. Thick vegetation. Very peaceable but not with other species.
Feeding: Omnivore.
Reproduction: In the courtship display, the male dances back and forth in front of the female. Every two months, the female gives birth to about 60 young that are often already more than 0.5 inch (1 cm) long.
Special Note: Not equipped with sperm storage (see p. 13). The variety with no golden body scales sometimes bites the fins off other fish.

Wrestling Halfbeak
Dermogenys pusilla

Characteristics: The males grow to about 2 inches (5 cm) and the more powerful females to 2.75 inches (7 cm). They have a peculiar body shape with a lengthened lower jaw. They swim in the top layer of the water.
Distribution: Southeast Asia.
Living Conditions: Aquarium of at least 20 gallons (76 L). Hard water, 75-86°F (24-30°C). Slight water movement. They need a few plants for protection. Males are very aggressive toward one another, so keep just one male with several females. Friendly with other fish.
Feeding: Small live food for young. Dry food for adults.
Reproduction: About every five weeks the females give birth to up to 50 young.
Special Note: The males are recognizable by the colored, slightly thickened anal fin.

Celebes Halfbeak
Nomorhamphus liemi

Characteristics: Males grow as long as two inches (5 cm), females to 3.5 inches (9 cm).
Distribution: Sulawesi (Indonesia). They live in the upper half of the water.
Living Conditions: Aquarium of at least 20 gallons (76 L). Hard water, 71–75°F (22–24°C). Slight current. Need large plants. Males are very aggressive toward one another, so keep just one male with several females. Peaceable with other fish that are not too small.
Feeding: Lots of frozen food.
Reproduction: The up to 25 young are already nearly 1 inch (2 cm) long at birth. Separate them in a nursery aquarium after a day to prevent parental harrassment.
Special Note: Their body configuration suggests a predatory life. Do not keep with fish under 0.75 inch (2 cm).

Questions About Lifestyle and Breeding Forms

I have read that live-bearers are school fish. Do I have to keep them in a school?

The schooling of the peaceable species (see the portraits on pp. 14 through 17) is surely the most appropriate living condition for the fish. In addition, that allows you to observe the varied and fascinating behavior repertory of this type of fish. A hierarchy will develop within the school. The male at the front of the school (known as the alpha male) is easy to spot because he is more colorful than the subordinate males. In addition, he is always the first one to appear at feeding. Keeping fish in schools, and even in pairs, entails the unavoidable disadvantage of reproduction.

Can I keep live-bearers with other fish?

Since most species of live-bearers are peaceable, they can easily associate with other live-bearers that are not too closely related and with other peaceable fish species. With swordtails and halfbeaks, though, the males are so aggressive toward one another that either just one male, or four to five males per species, can be kept in each aquarium.

There are so many species and breeding forms of live-bearers that are almost never available in stores. When can I find them?

Many breeders specialize in wild forms. Check page 60 for some leads, and continue your search online if necessary. Fish are also swapped and sold at fish shows. If you visit several breeders in your area, you will surely find numerous breeding forms. Every pet shop has its own wholesalers, and the next aquarium shop you contact may be able to offer different live-bearers. In addition, there are a few associations (see p. 60) that focus on breeding forms of live-bearers.

The Gold Molly—one of the Molly strains that have become popular in recent years.

Why is there a distinction between reproduction and breeding?
In fact, these are two separate topics. Reproduction is understood to mean the reproduction of the fish with no particular goal in mind. You let your guppies reproduce when you allow them free rein in the aquarium. Breeding involves a purpose, such as a particularly attractive fin shape. Through selective breeding, the breeder attempts to pass on a specific characteristic on to the young.

I would like to keep several species of live-bearers in an aquarium. Do they cross with one another?
Any time you keep males and females of the same species together, crosses are an exception because partners of the same type are usually preferred. Guppies and Mollies are capable of cross-

ing, but that produces only infertile males. Platys and Swordtails cross and can produce undesired mixes that are capable of reproduction.

I keep seeing the name Molly, but there is no fish species that goes by that name. What are Mollies?
The term Molly designates three species of the Poeciliidae: the Sailfin Molly (*Poecilia velifera*, see p. 15), the Short-finned Molly (*Poecilia sphenops*, see p. 15), and the Sailfin Molly (*Poecilia latipinna*). They are called Molly probably because they once went by the scientific name of *Mollienesia*.

Where does the name Halfbeak come from?
These fish have a very long lower jaw. This is an adaptation to their manner of eating. They live under the surface of the water and catch insects that swim on top of the water.

Harro Hieronimus

MY TIPS FOR YOU

Live-bearers — A Joy for Everyone

I can recommend live-bearers to everyone who enjoys keeping an aquarium:

➤ If you have children, then you should choose the breeding types that are easy to care for. They provide children with their first steps as aquarists. The children can experience the wonder of birth up close.

➤ If you are a beginner with aquariums, the simple breeding forms are a great choice because they will give you some valuable experience. You can also keep these fish in a community aquarium.

➤ If you are already an experienced aquarist, you can choose the more demanding wild forms from among the many breeding forms.

➤ Pros will find a challenge in the realm of selective breeding with live-bearers.

Appropriate Accommodations

A Comfortable Aquarium

Before buying your live-bearers, their new home has to be set up properly and checked out for two to three weeks. A number of aquariums and high-tech accessories are available in pet shops. I will explain what to look for so you can select the right materials for your fish.

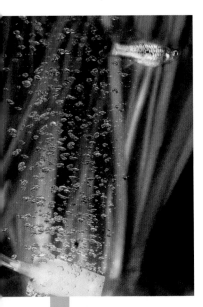

> *Good aeration provides adequate oxygen inside the aquarium.*

The Right Aquarium

Pet shops offer aquariums made of glass or plastic. Glass is better, because plastic can scratch easily. The panes of glass are glued into place with silicone rubber which discourages algae growth in the joints. When you buy an aquarium, make sure that it has no scratches or chips.

➤ **Size:** The larger the aquarium, the more stable its water quality (see p. 26). An aquarium for continuous residency by fish must be no smaller than 15 gallons (57 L). This is the type of aquarium commonly available measuring 24 × 12 × 12 inches (60 × 30 × 30 cm) (length × width × height). Exceptions are aquariums for breeding or for very small fish such as dwarf toothcarps, which grow to a maximum length of 1 inch (3 cm) or so. Once a guppy reaches 2 inches (5 cm), it is no longer a small fish. You must observe a number of rules in selecting the proper aquarium. One basic rule dictates that the length of the tank must be ten times as long and five times as wide as the body length of the longest fish. For guppies, an aquarium with a length of 24 inches (60 cm) is adequate. Swordtails and Sailfin Mollies reach a length of 4 inches (10 cm), so the ideal length of the aquarium would be at least 40 inches (100 cm). Aquariums commonly found in stores generally measure 36 × 12 × 24 inches (90 × 30 × 60 cm), with a capacity of 45 gallons (170 L). Whether or not this capacity is adequate depends on the number of fish kept in it, for there must be two quarts of water for every inch of fish (1 liter per centimeter of fish). See page 44 for further information.

➤ **Weight:** An aquarium of this size is tremendously heavy. Seventy gallons (250 L) of water by itself weighs about 550 pounds (250 kg). With substrate, decoration, plants, and accessories, this can quickly amount to 660 pounds (300 kg) or more. With this kind of weight, the support obviously has to be

1 Filter

Depending on size, an inside (up to about 45 gallons/170 L) or an outside filter is needed. It should have the capacity to filter the contents of the aquarium twice every hour. The filter must operate around the clock.

2 Heater

The heater needs to provide only about 2 watts per gallon (1/2 watt per liter) of water. For the proper performance, make sure that the heater is installed according to instructions and that the current washes around it.

3 Lighting

An aquarium needs a lighting source, small fluorescent aquarium bulbs or large halogen metal vapor lamps. The strength of the light should be about 4 watts per gallon (1 watt per liter) of aquarium contents.

CHECKLIST

Basic Equipment

For an aquarium of at least 24 inches (60 cm) in length made of glass and held together with silicone rubber, you will need the following:

✔ **Pad:** Usually made of felt or Styrofoam, the same size as the aquarium; it is placed under the aquarium so that no pebbles or similar items on the surface can force their way through the bottom pane.

✔ **Backdrop:** This increases the appearance of depth in aquariums that are placed next to a wall.

✔ **Cover:** At least a pane of glass should be used to cover the top of the aquarium to keep the fish from jumping out and the water from evaporating; often the cover has built-in lighting.

✔ **Lighting:** Aquariums need artificial lighting because natural daylight is not enough. Besides, excessive sunlight leads to algae growth.

✔ **Heat:** You must use a heater and a thermostat to regulate the temperature properly; nearly all live-bearers need a heated aquarium.

✔ **Filter:** The filter must be strong enough to cleanse the water and should turn over the water about twice every hour.

strong, preferably one made specifically for holding up an aquarium. You should have storage space below in which filters, electrical connections, food, and other accessories are kept. A foam rubber pad between the aquarium and the support helps protect the glass from breakage. You should also check the carrying capacity of your floor before setting up an aquarium of this weight.

Normally residential floors have a carrying capacity of 365 to 460 pounds per square yard (200 to 250 kg per square meter). If you have any doubt or live in an older house, consult a structural engineer before setting up an aquarium.

An Appropriate Location

Place the aquarium so that it does not get too much direct sunlight because that could cause considerable algae growth. Algae interfere with water quality. Two to three hours of sunshine daily are enough.

Most live-bearers do not mind lots of activity in front of the aquarium. Therefore, your aquarium can be placed in an area that you have to pass through a lot, for example near a door. Aquariums are also suitable for use as room dividers.

Where Do You Buy an Aquarium?

Pet shops offer a broad selection of aquariums. They often sell economically priced, prepackaged sets, too. However, I advise you to purchase aquariums and technical accessories individually. Individual sets are more costly than prepackaged ones, but they give you a greater choice and you can match the pieces to one another. In addition, prepackaged sets are usually sold without instructions. In any case, beginners should get plenty of advice about which aquarium is appropriate for the intended location and the fish that will inhabit it. One further advantage: you can always go back to the pet shop owner with your questions and problems.

Prepackaged sets can work well as breeding or nursery aquariums. If you already have experience, prepackaged sets can be very helpful. You can use them to supply miss-

Mickey Mouse Platys have one large and two small black spots.

TIP

Paying Attention to Safety

➤ Technical accessories are connected to an electrical current. Any time electricity and water come into contact with one another, a dangerous situation can result. Before performing any work in the aquarium on the accessories, disconnect the plug.

➤ Use only those heaters with protection against overheating; heaters without this protection can explode.

➤ You should install a surge protector (a separate plug-in). It automatically cuts off the power in case of a power surge.

Butterfly Goodeids belong to the Goodeidae family. These peaceable fish are easy to keep. About every eight weeks the females give birth to up to 50 large young. This species also eats algae.

ing or inadequate accessories, such as the filter.

Additional Equipment

➤ After a short while, fine algae grow on the inside of the aquarium glass, and they interfere with visibility. Algae scrapers and magnets, or a sponge, can be used to remove them. As you do so, make sure that pebbles or sand are not between the rubbing surface and the glass, or you will end up scratching the glass. You need a net any time you have to remove a fish from the aquarium, for example when you want to examine it or move it to a different place. If you have several aquariums, you should use a separate net for each one to keep from spreading diseases. Even with little fish, the net should be of a size that is easy to move through the water. The right-size net will make catching fish easier. It is easier still with two nets.

➤ For regular water changes, you need a hose and a bucket for draining the water and adding fresh water at the appropriate temperature. With large aquariums, you can save a lot of running around if a hose feeds directly into a drain and a hose for fresh water is attached to a faucet. You should use the hoses for only the aquarium.

➤ Exterior filters are especially appropriate for aquariums of 44 gallons (170 L) and larger; inside filters can be used for aquariums up to about 65 gallons (246 L). Many exterior filters combine the filter with a heater.

➤ A timer switch helps in setting the daylight to the necessary 10 to 12 hours. This is a requirement for proper plant growth.

Water Quality

In an aquarium, the fish have no way of escaping their habitat. They depend on you to provide the appropriate water for the aquarium.

To accomplish this, you should be familiar with the most important water values. They are easy to measure.

> *With Variegated Platys—here in coral color—the central fin rays are noticeably elongated.*

pH Value

This is a measurement of the acid-base content of the water. If the pH value is below 7, the water is acidic. If the acid-base content of the water is in a state of equilibrium, the water is neutral and the pH value is 7. Nearly all live-bearers in their natural environment live in hard water—so they do well in hard tap water. Thus, the pH level should always be over 7. It would be best to learn the pH of your tap water. Any necessary adjustments to the pH level can be made with products available at your local pet supply store.

Water Hardness

There are two types of hardness:

➤ The overall hardness is given in ppm. Water up to 125 ppm is considered soft; up to 200 ppm, medium-hard; up to 300 ppm, hard, and over 300 ppm, very hard.

➤ Carbonate hardness is expressed in kH. It stabilizes the pH value and therefore

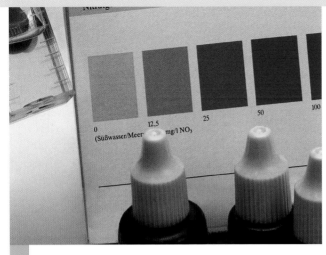

> *Performing the most important water tests is quick and easy using the test sets that are available on the market.*

should not be below 4°kH. If carbonate hardness is too low, additives available from pet shops can be used.

The Nitrogen Cycle

This is a chemical process in the water through which nitrogen compounds that are poisonous to fish are converted to less toxic substances.

➤ After you have set up the aquarium with plants, it must be in operation for two to three weeks until this process is in effect; then you can put in the fish. After setup, there is a high concentration of ammonia in the water—a toxic nitrogen compound. Bacteria from the air that settle in the filter break it down into nitrite, which is very poisonous to the fish. Still other bacteria that likewise inhabit the filter use it to form nitrates, which are toxic to fish only in high concentrations. Plants readily absorb this substance.

The fish may be put in only when no further nitrite can be detected in the water. Test kits are available in pet shops.
➤ The nitrogen cycle takes place even in an aquarium that has been broken in. The ammonia then comes from the excretions of the fish, from food remains, and from decomposing plants. The bacterial cultures in the filter can break down everything, though, as long as you help them with regular water changes (see p. 52).

Algae quickly become established in a newly set up aquarium. You will find out what to do in this case on pages 31 and 50.

TIP

How to Measure Water Quality

Specialty shops offer easy-to-use droplet and stick tests for the five pH values, overall and carbonate hardness, and nitrite and nitrate values.

➤ Titration tests: Drops of the test fluid are added to a specific amount of water. The color change indicates the value.

➤ Strip test: You dip the strip into the water and compare it with a color scale. Modern strip tests can indicate all five values at the same time.

Setting Up the Aquarium

An aquarium filled with nothing but colorful fish is not a beautiful sight. Pet shops offer a great variety of accessories.

Backdrop

A number of attractive backdrops contribute a particularly attractive decorative element. There are some that are stuck to the outside of the back panel of the aquarium—even photographic backgrounds that depict scenes from the natural habitat. For aquariums at least as large as $36 \times 12 \times 16$ inches ($90 \times 30 \times 40$ cm) there are also three-dimensional backgrounds that are joined to the inside back wall of the aquarium. They take up room, but they do look very realistic.

Substrate

Several types of substrate are available on the market. The usual one is fine-grained, unbleached gravel with no sharp edges. However, you can also get lava gravel and coarse gravel. Sand is less appropriate because it can clump together and form areas of decay. The darker the color of the substrate, the better the colors of the fish look.

The substrate should be at least 1 to 2.75 inches (3 to 7 cm) deep. To create an appearance of spaciousness, install it so it slopes upward toward the rear.

Decoration

Pet shops offer a broad selection of decorative items. **Roots and stones** added to an aquarium must not affect

> *Plants turn the aquarium into a real miniature biotope.*

TIP

Taking Care of Plants

➤ When you install plants, you have to make sure that the roots point straight down.

➤ Many stem plants need to be trimmed regularly because they spread too much. You can also carefully use scissors to remove unsightly leaves from leafy plants.

➤ If necessary, you can encourage plant growth by adding fertilizers containing iron (available in specialty shops).

➤ In addition to adequate light conditions, dissolved carbon dioxide (CO_2) is good for plants.

the water quality. In other words, pieces of oak or decorative pine roots picked up from a swamp are taboo. They give off pigments (humic acids) in the water that live-bearers cannot tolerate. For stone decorations, you can use any well-washed stone free of sharp edges. You can keep a stone structure from falling apart by gluing the stones into the desired shape with silicone rubber.

Plants in the Aquarium

Plants support a healthy climate in the aquarium. The choice depends on the size of the aquarium and the plants' light requirements. For a brightly illuminated aquarium, fanwort (*Cabomba*) and burhead or Amazon sword plant (*Echinodorus*) are good choices. You can use *Cryptocoryne* or flowering Anubias (*Anubias*) in an aquarium that does not receive much light. In planting, place the taller plants in the background and on the sides, and use shorter plants toward the front. That will produce spaciousness and depth, and you can easily observe your fish in the ample swimming area in the foreground. Be sure to

Plants improve water quality, so they should be part of any aquarium that is home to many fish.

select plants that root in the substrate. Floating plants such as the water lettuce (*Pistia statiotes*) block too much light for the other plants. The young offspring of the live-bearers have a better chance of survival if they can hide among thick, fine plants. Especially good choices include the various *Cabomba* and *Myriophyllum* species plus Mayaca fluviatilis, hornwort, and Canadian waterweed. Java moss (*Vesicularia dubyana*) also works well.

Questions About Technical Details and Setup

How long should I keep the aquarium illuminated?

The average duration of lighting should be between 10 and 14 hours (at least 1 watt per quart/liter of water with higher-wattage lamps, and 0.75 watt per quart/liter of water with lower wattages). If you use a timer, you can program a midday break without illumination; the fish and plants will quickly get used to it. Working people make good use of this because the light can be left on longer at night. Three hours of normal daylight (without direct sun) is about equivalent to one hour of medium-intensity illumination. So if you can institute a midday break of three hours, you can keep the light on for two hours longer in the evening.

Fluorescent tubes come in various colors. Which one should I choose?

With aquariums, three colors are most often used: hard white, soft white, and GroLux (reddish). Hard white corresponds most closely to daylight and is the best choice for the plants. GroLux accentuates the red colors in the fish but is not as good for the plants. The ideal combination is one or two hard white tubes with one reddish one.

What is meant by a T5 lamp?

This refers to fluorescent tubes with a particularly high light output and about twice the life expectancy of normal tubes (T8). They are particularly effective in encouraging plant growth, and the aquarium can be illuminated for one or two hours less. T5 lamps fit into every normal fixture for fluorescent bulbs.

How do I determine the characteristics of my tap water?

Your local water department may be able to tell you the specific values. A phone call

Mollies are good algae eaters and do a fine job of keeping the aquarium plants clean.

should suffice. In order to facilitate providing this information, many municipal water departments have their water analyses posted on the Internet. The analyses are listed on the home page of your water supplier (indicated on your water bill). You could even ask your local pet store.

All of a sudden, there is a lot of green algae in my aquarium. Is something wrong with my filter?
This may be one reason why green algae are reproducing quickly. However, the filter may be too small for your aquarium (it needs to filter the water twice every hour), or it may need servicing (see p. 51 for service intervals). Also check the location of the aquarium. If it is close to a window and in direct sun, green algae will grow. Another reason may be excessively high nitrogen content because of an overabundance of fish or too few plants. As an emergency measure, I advise you to clean the filter or replace it if necessary, reduce the duration and intensity of the illumination,

and place the aquarium in a darker location. In addition, you should change the water weekly, restrict feeding to a certain time, and install fast-growing plants.

I have washed newly purchased substrate several times, and yet the water is still cloudy. Is this dangerous?
Even though the substrate has been washed, it still contains fine suspended particles. This produces mild clouding and is one reason why fish should be introduced to an aquarium only a few days after setup—after the filter has removed the particles.

I really like bamboo. Can I use it for decoration?
Bamboo has no effect on water values, so it can be used for decoration. However, you will have to weight it down with stones because it is very light. You will have to seal the cut edges of the bamboo stalks with silicone so that no algae or bacteria can take hold.

Harro Hieronimus

MY TIPS FOR YOU

Putting the Aquarium into Operation

➤ Make sure that the aquarium has suffered no damage. Set it onto a cabinet or tabletop. Place a soft underlay such as a Styrofoam or felt pad between the aquarium and the tabletop.

➤ Thoroughly wash the substrate and put it into the aquarium.

➤ Install the filter and the heater, but do not turn them on yet.

➤ Fill the aquarium halfway with water. Then put in the plants.

➤ Fill the aquarium the rest of the way, start the filter and the heater, put the cover into place, and turn on the light.

Test the water after three weeks. Normally the fish can move in because the bacteria necessary for the nitrogen cycle (see p. 27) have had a chance to establish themselves.

Acclimation Program

Selection and Purchase

You can make your first mistakes as soon as you buy some fish. Impulse buying is dangerous. You spot some fish with unusual fin shapes or colors and buy them, and only on the way home does it dawn on you that you already have enough fish in your aquarium. Reflect first, and then buy.

> *The red Wagtail Platy is one of the most beloved breeding forms.*

Where Should You Buy Fish?

➤ The first trip should be to the pet shop. During your visit, form an impression of whether everything is clean and neat, if the front panes of the aquariums are free of algae, and whether there are any dead or sick fish to be seen. If any of these points is not in order, do not buy from this shop. Still, a pet shop is not immune to diseases. An aquarium with a sign stating that nothing inside it is for sale is a sign of conscientiousness.

➤ The more specific your desires, the more dealers you will have to visit to find your dream fish. Still, you are unlikely to find in a store some wild or exotic breeding forms of Guppies, for example, even after an intensive search. In that case, contact the relevant associations (see Addresses, p. 60). Every year there are shows where rare species and breeding forms are offered for sale.

➤ Want ads in association publications or on the Web pages of the associations often produce results.

Quarantine

In pet shops, fish pass through numerous stages and come into contact with many other fish. They are thus always susceptible to contracting some disease. Even if the fish appear healthy on the outside, they may already be sick. So if you put the newly purchased fish right into the aquarium with numerous other fish, the whole population may become sick. You can prevent this with a quarantine aquarium. This type of aquarium must already be set up before you purchase the new fish. There must be no detectable ammonia or nitrite in the water. In this instance, only low-maintenance plastic plants are acceptable. A little substrate such as a thin layer of sand, a vibrator pump, and modest lighting are adequate. Naturally, only a few fish should be accommodated here. Depending on the size of the fish, aquariums of about 5 gallons (16 L) or more will work satisfactorily. If an illness crops up here, you need to deal with only the new arrivals. The quarantine should last two to three weeks. Thereafter, dry out the whole setup and disinfect everything.

Combinations of Fish

You will almost always want to keep live-bearers with other fish. The question arises about the species that have similar requirements

> *During the courtship display, the male Humpback Limia swims tirelessly around the female until mating occurs.*

Health Check: How to Recognize a Healthy Fish

Points to Check	Desired Appearance
Nutritional Status	A rounded belly profile is a sign of good nutritional status.
Scales	The scales must lie close to the body, and none should be standing up.
Breathing	The fish must breathe calmly, without gulping convulsively for air.
Fins and Skin	The fins must be clear and show no tears. They should not be clamped tight to the body. Skin and fins should be free of whitish spots and cloudy areas.
Eyes	The eyes must exhibit no cloudy layers.
Behavior	The fish should not rock to and fro or rub against items in the aquarium. If a fish remains apart from the group, it is a sign of illness. Many live-bearers perform their first courtship display at the pet shop.
Water Color	A yellow, green, or blue tint to the water is a sign of some treatment; you should avoid buying these fish.

for water quality, temperature, and planting. They must also pose no danger to the live-bearers. Since there is a large selection available, at this point I can offer you just a few tips.

➤ Live-bearers are easy to place into association with one another. A trio of Swordtails (one male and two females), a couple of male Guppies and two females, and a male Black Molly will get along fine with one another and with other fish in a large aquarium. Only Swordtails and Platys should not be kept in the same aquarium because they interbreed (see p. 19).

➤ Never buy only two or three male Swordtails or Mollies. They are very aggressive toward males of the same species and fight violently. After a short time, you will have only one male left.

A Couple of Representative Combinations: Live-bearers generally prefer the middle regions of the water. Bronze Cories (*Corydoras*) or Bushynose Plecs (*Ancistrus*) are candidates for the bottom; the latter also help keep the glass and plants free of algae. In addition to these, you can put in a mating pair, or three males with five to six females, of the Australian Dwarf Rainbow Fish (*Melanotaenia maccullochi*). For the upper layers of the water, another appropriate live-bearer is the Southeast Asian Halfbeak. To populate the middle water layers further, you can use many bony fishes, such as the Bleeding Heart Tetra (*Hyphessobrycon erythrostigma*) and the Zebrafish (*Danio rerio*) (a school fish), and the Ticto

Guppies get along well with other fish.

CHECKLIST

Proper Acclimation

✔ If the aquarium is your first one of this type, it must be set up and broken in for at least three weeks (see p. 31) before putting fish into it.

✔ After introducing the fish into the aquarium, observe them closely. They should eat normally and behave naturally.

✔ In the first days, the new fish may still be skittish, so you should put off working in the aquarium.

✔ Before putting the new fish into the aquarium, feed the current residents to distract them and allay their hunger. After feeding them, slip in the new fish.

✔ Remember that you generally buy young fish in a shop. In order for them to develop properly, they need an adequately large aquarium.

✔ Fairly thick planting offers the newcomers protection in the early days. They will still have to venture out for food; otherwise, they may become sick.

✔ After three days at the most, the new fish should behave like the others.

1 Transporting Fish

You will get your fish in a plastic bag, which you should have the dealer wrap in newspaper. Transport the package on its side; the greater water surface will allow more oxygen into the water. In the summer, don't keep the bag in the car, for it heats up too quickly inside.

2 Transferring the Fish

The bag with the new fish is placed into the quarantine aquarium and suspended for twenty minutes to equalize the temperature. Then pour half of the water out of the bag and replace it with water from the aquarium. After another twenty minutes you can release the fish into the aquarium.

Barb (*Puntius ticto*). Further choices include Papondetta Blue-eye (genus *Pseudomugil*) and Three-spot Gourami (*Trichogaster trichopterus*).

If you are not interested in breeding or even hope to prevent it so the aquarium does not become too full, you can put in several small or two or three larger Angelfish. Among other things, they eat young fish. For further examples of combinations, see page 45.

Important: Under no circumstances should live-bearers, especially Guppies, be placed with Tiger Barbs. The latter bite the others on the long tail fins and can injure or even kill them. The same applies to Blackspotted Pufferfish and some types of loaches.

In the first few days, you need to observe fish closely that have recently been placed together. At the first sign of problems, you must be prepared to intervene, for example, by separating the combatants.

Even before buying fish, it makes sense to mention to the pet shop owner the kinds of fish you would like to place together and find out if they will tolerate one another. In case of problems, a good dealer will accept the return of a fish.

Behavior Interpreter
Live-bearers

Do you understand the language of live-bearers?
Here you will learn what your charges are expressing
through their behavior and the proper way to
react to it →.

> Two Butterfly Goodeids cuddle
close to one another as they
swim along.
>
> **?** The two fish are in the
process of mating.
> **→** Set up a nursery aquarium.
The young will be born in
two months.

> The Guppies hang just beneath
the surface of the water and
gulp for air.
>
> **?** There is not enough oxygen
in the water.
> **→** Change some of the water,
check the filter, and clean it.

One Sailfin Molly male is fighting with another male.

? The dominant male is lording it over the weaker one.

➡ Keep several males of this species; that way only one of them will be attacked.

The Platys always swim together in the community aquarium.

? They are school fish, and that is the way they feel most comfortable.

➡ This is a natural behavior.

A Marble Molly keeps sucking on the bottom.

? As an algae eater, it searches the bottom for edibles.

➡ Do not interfere. This is a natural and useful behavior.

The Sailfin Molly is spreading its fins.

? A male is performing a courtship display for a female.

➡ When the female gives in, they will soon mate.

39

Courtship Displays and Reproduction

As a beginner, you will likely keep colorful breeding forms of Guppies. If you keep males and females of the same species, you will soon find yourselves with young fish on your hands without any intervention on your part. Breeding forms usually reproduce readily. In contrast, not even specialists experience consistent success with breeding wild forms.

Impressive Courtship Behavior

Many live-bearers perform a real courtship dance before mating. Male Guppies first appear before the females with fanned and then with folded fins. Male Swordtails dart back and forth in sickle-shaped swoops in front of the females (sickle dance). Male Mollies spread their fins almost to the point of tearing and place themselves at an angle in front of the females. Mating occurs only when the courting pleases the female.

Mating

With live-bearers the eggs are fertilized inside the womb. The males first have to transfer their sperm. In this respect, there are some differences among individual families of fish.

With live-bearing Tooth-carps, the males have a modified anal fin, the gonopodium. If you look closely at young fish, you will see that a couple of weeks after birth, some fish, namely the males,

The gravid spot on this female Guppy is clearly visible.

TIP

What to Do with the Offspring?

If you keep a mating pair of live-bearers in the aquarium, you will unavoidably end up with offspring.

➤ Ask friends and acquaintances in advance if they are interested in having some of the fry.

➤ Once your excess offspring have developed their colors, you can try to get your pet shop owner to buy them.

Even if you want to breed young fish, you should keep only the strong, fast-growing ones and eliminate the others (see p. 57).

1 Identifying Male Guppies

By using a magnifying glass, you can identify in male Guppies a thickening of the middle rays of the anal fin; the area of the fin also becomes cloudy. These rays grown into a penis-like reproductive organ, the gonopodium. It is fully developed after about two months.

2 Identifying Female Guppies

Female Guppies soon develop a small but clearly visible dark spot in the area of the anal fin; later on it develops into the so-called gravid spot. This spot is visible starting around the age of three weeks. After five weeks, female Guppies are rounder and somewhat larger than the males.

have three rays in their anal fin that become thickened and elongated. These rays have a complex structure that is peculiar to each species; they almost always end in a hook. However, this hook is visible only under a microscope. The male uses it to hook into the female's genital orifice while transferring sperm.

Goodeids and Halfbeaks also have a gonopodium for sperm delivery. With these species, only the forward rays (or the rear ones, in the case of *Hemirhamphodon* Halfbeaks) of the anal fin are slightly thickened and shortened. The male uses them to form a sort of chute for fertilization.

The Four-Eyed Fish and Line Toothcarps have a gonopodium resembling that of the live-bearing Tooth-carps, but it forms a proper tube and can be moved in just one direction—either left or right. For example, a male whose gonopodium moves toward the left can fertilize only females whose genital orifice is located on the right—and conversely.

The Birth of the Young

After fertilization, the eggs develop inside the female's body. This altered state is visible in many species. The female develops what is known as a gravid spot, a large, dark area in the anal region (see photo, p. 40). With Guppies, it is possible to see the eyes of the young ones shining through shortly before birth.

Breeding forms in particular give birth regularly around every four weeks. With Guppies, Mollies, and Platys, this can involve about

50 young and with sword-tails, over 100. At quick intervals, the young are born as tiny balls that immediately unroll. Right after giving birth, the females are badgered by the males, which put on the courtship display and try to fertilize the females again. Shortly after giving birth, the females emit special scents known as pheromones. They cause the males to repeat the courtship dance energetically. Even though the live-bearers have sperm storage (see p. 13), this ensures that the next litter is properly fertilized. Do not interfere with the males. After a couple of days, the pheromones will cease. As a result, the pronounced courtship behavior will stop by itself.

Raising the Young

Immediately after birth, the young fish swim away from their mother. Since in the wild as well as in the aquarium they are prey to many animals—in many cases even to their parents—they take shelter among the plants.

➤ If you want to raise all the young fry, you must remove them and transfer them to a special aquarium. This type of nursery aquarium should not be too small. Ten gallons (38 L) will suffice for 40 guppies up to 1 inch (2 cm) or for 40 Mollies or Sword-tails up to 1.5 inches (3 cm). All you need for accessories is a heater, a small filter, and especially thick planting that takes up about one-third of the aquarium. I advise against the tiny, little, floating nursery boxes. The young fish will not grow properly inside them.

➤ If you want the young fish to grow up under "natural" conditions, in other words in the community aquarium, you should offer them ample

➤ *A female guppy and her already half-grown offspring.*

see p. 13

TIP

Preventing Unwanted Offspring

Nearly all live-bearers give birth to young in regular intervals of about four weeks when females and males are kept together. However, it is possible to prevent this reproduction by doing the following:

➤ Keep only males. For reasons of competitiveness, this requires at least six fish.

➤ Keep some fish that eat fry. Appropriate choices include the Redchin Panchax. In larger aquariums, peaceable Cichlids such as Angelfish are appropriate.

opportunities to hide, such as thick water plants or caves under rocks, where only the youngsters can fit.

What to Watch for in Raising Young Fish

Immediately after birth, the young of live-bearers are independent and able to swim. However, they need food right away, and they produce a lot of waste. As a result, you need to devote a lot of energy to caring for the water. This involves water changes and conscientious removal of decayed matter left over from repeated daily feedings. The cleaner the water, the faster the young fish grow, and the more resistant they will be to disease. After a short time, the nursery aquarium will be too small for the young fish. As soon as they are longer than 1 inch (2 cm), you can transfer them to a large community aquarium with peaceable fish species such as Corydoras and Rainbow Fish, plus their parents. Make sure that the community aquarium does not become too crowded.

Feeding the Young Fish:
One good food for young

> *A young Butterfly Goodeid spots the light coming from the outer world.*

fish is freshly hatched *Artemia nauplii* (see p. 48). However, you can also use fine dry food and Mikro. Mikro is tiny worms; you can get the breeding base and breeding instruction from a breeder or from the Internet. A diet with as much variety as possible has something to offer everyone. Up to the age of four weeks, young fish need to be fed three times a day; up to three months, twice a day; and thereafter, once a day like adults.

CHECKLIST

Necessities for Raising Young Fish

✔ As many fine, feathery plants as possible among which the young can take shelter

✔ A small aquarium with aeration and lots of plants if you remove the females

✔ Frequent water changes in the nursery aquarium so that the young fish grow properly

✔ Food that is small enough so that even the young fish can eat

✔ Several feedings per day

✔ Avoid using nursery boxes; they are too small, and the young fish do not grow properly inside them

Questions About Purchase and Socialization

? I would like to bring some fish home from a distant city and will be on the road for 10 hours. Is that feasible?

That should be fine. Tell the seller how long your trip will take. The seller can put the fish into a larger bag and fill it with oxygen. Newspaper will work for providing warmth and blocking visibility. In the summer and winter, you can also ask the dealer for a Styrofoam box or bring along an insulated bag like that used for transporting frozen goods.

? Do I really need a quarantine aquarium for my new fish?

If these are the first fish in your aquarium, you do not need a quarantine aquarium. However, if you already have an aquarium populated with fish, in the interest of the health of the old-timers, you should put the newcomers into a quarantine aquarium. Even if you buy from an absolutely reliable source, such as from an acquaintance, that person may have some disease in his or her aquariums without even knowing it.

? How many fish can I put into my 15-gallon (57 L) aquarium?

You must observe these three rules as you put in fish. 1) The accessories displace water—about 10 percent of capacity. So your aquarium really provides only about 13.5 gallons (51 L) of water that can be occupied. 2) An adult fish needs 1 quart/liter of water. A male Guppy that is 1 inch (2.5 cm) long needs just about 3 quarts/liters of water; a female Guppy that is 2 inches (5 cm) long needs 5 quarts/liters. 3) The tank must be about ten times as long and five times as wide as the eventual length of the largest fish. No fish longer than 2.5 inches (6 cm) should be placed into your tank. If your aquarium is suited to

This dog-eared Swordtail shows that there are some biting fish present.

four mating pairs of Guppies, for example, each pair needs 8 quarts/liters of water. So four pairs need 32 quarts/liters. Since they reproduce, put in three Redchin Panchax. They eat young Guppies. One Redchin Panchax measures 2 inches (5 cm), so three need 15 quarts/liters of water.

? I have Tiger Barbs and Zebrafish, and I would also like to put in three mating pairs of Deltatail Guppies. Will that work?
No, I advise against it. Tiger Barbs pick at all long fins and will bite off the tail fins not only from the male Guppies but from all long-finned fish. In addition, these species have different pH requirements, so they do not go well together.

? I already have some Red Neons and Agassiz's Apistos. Will Guppies or Swordtails fit in with them?
Both the Red Neons and the Agassiz's Apistos are freshwater fish, and they like slightly acidic water. Swordtails, Platys, and Mollies, on the other hand, come from

hard-water regions and are comfortable only in hard water. Guppies live in hard and soft water and can be combined with Neons and Agassiz's Apistos such as *Apistogramma agassizii*. However, the Guppies must not have been previously kept in water with added salt, as is usually the case in pet shops. Ask your pet shop owner about this and buy from only a store where no salt is added. The aquarium for this combination must hold at least 29 gallons (110 L).

? I have a 15-gallon (57 L) aquarium and would like to put in some Guppies. Should I get more males or females?
With such a small aquarium, you should consider if you really want to put in females. The offspring from just one female will very quickly overpopulate your aquarium. Six to eight males will continually perform the courtship display even without females and will provide you with a good view. They also live happily without females. In this quantity, no male will be oppressed by the others.

MY TIPS FOR YOU

Harro Hieronimus

Introducing Fish

➤ Ask the dealer from whom you buy your fish if salt is added to the water of the live-bearers. If so, you too have to put salt in at first and decrease the concentration through water changes over the course of several weeks.

➤ After installing the newcomers, pay attention to how the other fish react. If the new ones are attacked, put in a little food to distract the older fish.

➤ Do not put Deltatail Guppies in with particularly fast fish species such as Bleeding Heart Tetras. They will either eat the Guppies' food or you will have to put in so much food that the water will become contaminated.

➤ Select young fish because they are already accustomed to the water quality that live-bearers like.

Overall Health Program

What Live-bearers Eat

One factor that affects the well-being of your fish is proper nutrition. Improper or excessive food merely harms your fish. Variety in feeding is also important. Some wild forms are food specialists. Most breeding forms, though—the ones that are the subject of this book— will do just as well with a good commercial dry food as with live and frozen foods. Pet shops offer all kinds of foods.

In order to provide a little variety and the needed vitamins in your fishes' menu, I advise you to select dry food as the main food and provide additives of live or frozen food two to three times a week.

Types of Food

➤ **Dry Food:** This consists of flakes that are produced using a variety of ingredients. Several producers also offer special dried foods for particular species, such as Guppies. They are designed to promote growth and more attractive colors.

➤ **Live Food:** This includes red, black, and white mosquito larvae as well as the various species of water fleas. Gathering your own live food may be impractical or illegal because protected species are often living in the appropriate waters. You can buy a limited selection in packets that keep them fresh. Of course, these are treats.

➤ **Frozen Food:** This consists of frozen live food. There is quite a large selection.

Plant Food

All Mollies, like other live-bearers, are algae eaters in the wild. You can get special dry food made from plants for them. They will also eat all the algae in the aquarium. In order to provide some variety in their diet, you can give them scalded spinach (even frozen, but of course with no additives) or blanched lettuce leaves.

Raising Live Food

You can raise some live food yourself with no great expense. This includes especially the tiny *Artemia nauplii. A. nauplii* is a salt-water shrimp that lay small eggs in long-lasting form known as cysts. These long-lasting eggs are available in specialty shops. They are made to hatch by placing them in salt water at 75°F to 79°F (24–26°C) under strong ventilation for 24 to 48 hours. Then you carefully

➤ Nearly all live-bearers like all kinds of live food.

use a pipette to suck up the *A. nauplii* and feed them straight to the fish. Even large Guppies and Platys like this type of food.

> *Guppies are curious and greedy eaters. Give them only as much as they can eat in five minutes.*

Golden Rules of Feeding

	What You Should Do
How much food?	Always feed only as much as the fish will eat in a maximum of five minutes. Observe one day of fasting per week. Then the fish will scour the aquarium and clean it. Do not let them fool you. Fish that swim up to the glass when you approach are usually just curious, not hungry
What kind of food?	Provide a variety, and try to give the fish live food at least twice a week. Feed only fresh food that is still within the freshness date. Throw away any spoiled food.
When to feed?	Feed one hour after turning on the aquarium light. You should never feed shortly before turning off the light.
How often?	Feed adult live-bearers once a day. For young fish, see page 43.
What to look for?	Check to see if all fish are eating. Refusal to eat is a sign of illness.

Healthy with the Proper Care

Healthy, moderate feeding (see p. 49) plus regular care in the aquarium will help your fish feel good. It strengthens the fishes' immune system and their defenses.

A Couple of Rules:

➤ You should not put new arrivals in with your fish without first putting them into quarantine. Otherwise,

➤ An attractive pair of Black Mollies with a fork- or lyretail.

you risk an outbreak of disease.

➤ Food must not be kept improperly or too long. Dry food must be stored cool and dry, and a packet should be used up within six weeks of opening. Frozen food may be given lightly thawed, never fully thawed, and it must under no circumstances be refrozen once it has thawed.

➤ In case you accidentally give too much food, suck up the leftovers right away. Otherwise you will create an excess of nutrients and consequent algae growth.

Observing the Fish

Every day, perhaps at feeding time, take a few minutes to observe your fish. Unaccustomed behavior such as hiding, loss of appetite, or altered appearance, for example a thin coating on the fins, may be signs of a health problem (see p. 35).

Cleaning the Aquarium

In addition to changing the water (see p. 52), you also have to clean the glass. Algae can become attached to the glass as well as the plants and decorative objects. They get in quickly, especially in a newly set-up aquarium. Algae are usually a sign of too much nitrate or phosphate in the water, and they are helped along by excess light. Change the water more frequently, wash the filter, and reduce the intensity of the light. You can take control of the algae by cleaning the glass with algae scrapers, algae magnets, or a sponge. You can use snails such as Great Ramshorns in the struggle against algae. However, they eat holes in the plants when the algae are all gone.

Checking the Water

Normally, the water in the aquarium has no unpleasant odor.

➤ A fairly strong odor indicates a faulty routine for changing water. If the water smells even though you change it fairly frequently, you should check the number of fish. When the aquarium

Healthy Guppies have a curved belly profile. A pinched-in stomach is a clear sign of illness.

Taking Care of Fish

Try to carry out several steps at one time to avoid disturbing the fish needlessly.

Daily
✔ Feed the fish.
✔ Observe the fish for abnormal behavior.

Weekly
✔ Remove dead plant pieces.
✔ Remove algae from the glass. Avoid damaging silicone caulking with the algae scraper.

Every Two Weeks
✔ Replace about a third of the water with fresh tap water at the same temperature.
✔ When you change the water, also suck up any decayed matter.

As Necessary
✔ Clean the filter material, replace very dirty parts with new ones, rinse the rest under lukewarm water, and return to use.
✔ Empty the aquarium completely, clean the substrate, and put it back into place. This measure is required if the plants cease growing and small bubbles appear on the substrate. Do a complete cleaning at least once a year.

is crowded, the water should be changed more frequently than when the population is kept to the proper level. See page 44 for information on calculating the ideal number of fish.

➤ A yellowish hue is a warning sign that the water is too old and needs to be freshened. Driftwood discolors the water a lot. Since most livebearers do not come from areas in which humic substances are present in the water, driftwood has no place in your aquarium.

➤ In the case of milky cloudiness, the cause is tiny creatures (infusorians) that have reproduced explosively as a consequence of feeding the fish too much. To counter this condition, discontinue feeding for three days and replace a third of the water with fresh water.

Changing the Water

In spite of the filter and water plants, some harmful substances build up in the aquarium. Over the long run, they may be detrimental to the fish. I therefore recommend replacing about 30 percent (but never more than 50 percent) of the water with tap water at the same temperature at least every 14 days. Use a hose for the purpose. Place both ends of the hose into the aquarium. While submerged, lift one end slightly to allow the air to leave the hose. Cover one end with your thumb and move that end to a bucket that is lower than the aquarium.

Remove your thumb. The water will run into the bucket. This also allows you to siphon out decayed matter (leftover food, excretions, and plants). Remember to shut off the electrical devices during the process.

When You Need to Act

Often there are warning signs that are easy to overlook.
➤ A musty smell and a greenish or blackish coating on the still corners of the water surface are signs of blue algae. They are indications that the water needs to be changed.
➤ There may be several causes for dying plants, including neglected water changes.
➤ You especially need to check out the mechanical devices. They are capable of keeping the fishes' environment in proper order only if they are working properly. A defective light, a filter that runs poorly—all of these pose a direct threat to the life of your fish.

Necessary Measures

I recommend that you draw up a plan to follow. That way you are sure to forget nothing, and you avoid disturbing the fish unnecessarily. I have put together a recommended care schedule for you in the checklist on page 51.

Problems Due to Living Conditions

Outside influences can lead to outbreaks of disease.
➤ The temperature may drop due to heater malfunction.
➤ If the fish race around the tank and crash into the glass, the cause is almost always some kind of poisoning. Solvents and an excess of nicotine in the surrounding air are harmful to the fish. With nitrite or ammonia poisoning, which can occur in a newly set-up aquarium or with overcrowding, the fish often float right under the surface of the water even though ample oxygen is in the water.

➤ Regular water changes help keep your fish healthy.

Immediate First Aid in Emergencies

The Fish Are Gulping for Air

➤ **Immediately:** Replace a third of the aquarium water with fresh water at the same temperature.

Long Term: Regularly check the functioning of the filter, and clean or replace as needed. Install additional aeration. With newly set-up or crowded aquariums, reduce the population, check the nitrite content regularly, and add starter bacteria if there is too much nitrite.

Dampness Around the Aquarium

➤ **Immediately:** Check all hose connections to and from the aquarium and replace any defective connections. Check the silicone seams for tightness. If glued joints are defective, provide a new aquarium and make the changeover as quickly as possible. If necessary, temporarily keep everything in a bucket.

Long Term: To avoid damaging the silicone joints, use a sponge to clean the glass.

There Is a Dead Fish in the Aquarium

➤ **Immediately:** Use a net to remove the fish and examine it for signs of disease.

Long Term: Observe the aquarium carefully in the following days. The fish may have died of natural causes such as old age, or it may have died from disease. If other fish exhibit signs of illness, administer appropriate medications (see chart on p. 55).

Sudden, Excessive Green Algae Growth

➤ **Immediately:** Suspend feeding for at least three days, change the water, and clean or replace the filter as needed.

Long Term: Feed less and put in a few fast-growing plants such as hornwort or Canadian waterweed to restrict the nutrients in the water and starve out the algae. Change the water regularly.

The Fish Are Darting About Madly

➤ **Immediately:** Harmful substances have gotten into the water. Change half of the water and observe the fish closely; if necessary, perform further water changes.

Long Term: Avoid dangerous substances in the water. Air fresheners and excess cigarette smoke can be poisonous to fish. Water-soluble solvents from varnishes are particularly dangerous.

The Water Has a Greenish Tinge

➤ **Immediately:** A greenish tinge is due to tiny algae. Immediately suspend feeding for three days. Check the filter, and clean or replace if necessary. Provide illumination for only five to six hours during one week. Check for overcrowding.

Long Term: Give less food and change the water regularly. Use products from the pet shop to combat these floating algae.

The Most Common Diseases

Diseases can crop up even in a well-tended aquarium. By intervening early, you can minimize the harmful effects.

Recognizing Sick Fish
Many diseases can be identified by outward changes such as shifts in color and coatings on fins and body. A fish's behavior can also

> There must be no white areas on the fish's mouth.

indicate disease. Rocking in the water, clamped fins, withdrawal from the school, and wariness of objects are almost sure signs that a fish is sick. I can give you some general advice here. For more precise descriptions of diseases and how to treat them, though, please consult technical literature.

Pathogens
Pathogens include parasites, bacteria, and fungi. They get into the aquarium through carelessness, for example from new fish that have not been subjected to quarantine. **Fairly large parasites** such as *Icthyophthirius multifiliis* (White Spot) can be detected with the naked eye. Smaller parasites such as *Costia costia* can be identified only under the microscope. Most parasites can be treated successfully with an appropriate medication.

Many fungal diseases such as *Saprolegnia* (cotton mold) occur when fish are already weakened by other pathogens such as bacteria. In such instances, both diseases must be addressed.

Bacteria are present in large numbers in every aquarium. An external bacterial infestation, recognizable by means of cloudy coatings on fins and skin and a damaged surface, must be treated quickly, because some of these bacteria are very aggressive and reproduce quickly. Even 36 hours after the onset of an infection it may be too late for treatment. Thus you should always have a cure on hand in your fish medicine cabinet. Get advice from the pet shop owner. Internal bacterial infections are identifiable only by the symptoms; they include exophthalmia (goggle eye), ascites (hydroperitoneum: distended body with protruding scales), serious weight loss, and sores visible on the outside.

Worms can infest a fish's intestines. If left untreated, diseases caused by worms nearly always lead to the death of the fish.

Recognizing and Treating Diseases

Symptoms	Cause	Treatment
Cottonlike coating on skin and fins	*Saprolegnia* (cotton molds)	Carefully remove large accumulations with tweezers; apply medication from pet shop according to instructions.
White dots the size of grit on skin and fins	White Spot Disease caused by the *Icthyophthirius multifiliis* parasite (*Oodinium pillularis*)	Apply medication from pet shop according to instructions.
Fine, dot-shaped coating on body; fish rock and appear skittish	General illness caused by parasites that have gotten into the skin	Apply medication from pet shop according to instructions.
The fish keeps getting fatter, and the scales stand up	Ascites or hydroperitoneum caused by bacteria	Nearly impossible to treat. Isolate fish; if the condition worsens, put the fish out of its misery. As a preventive measure, improve the water quality by changing it.
Whitish areas on the body that break out suddenly	*Columnaris*, a species of bacteria	Apply medication from pet shop according to instructions.
Fins have white margins and decay from the inside	Bacterial fin rot	Apply medication from pet shop; treat quickly because the bacteria are very aggressive.
Fish are losing lots of weight even though they are eating and droppings appear normal	Wrong food; in worst case, fish tuberculosis	Check food for suitability. In case of severe weight loss, put fish out of its misery.
Pale, transparent droppings	Intestinal worms	Treatment with 5% Flubenol (prescription from vet), dribbled onto frozen food
Red worms hanging out the fish's anus	*Camallanus* nematodes	10% Concurat (from vet), soak 1 g in 2 teaspoons (10 mL) of water and dribble onto frozen food.
Crooked spine in young fish	Inherited spinal defect	No treatment; keep fish from reproducing; best to euthanize them to avoid passing on spinal deformity

Questions on Care and Diseases

Should I treat a sick fish in the quarantine aquarium?
If you discover a sick fish, you should treat the entire crew because most pathogens spread through the water very quickly. The only time you should treat a sick fish separately in the quarantine aquarium is with noninfectious diseases, such as *Saprolegnia* (see chart, p. 55). Otherwise, the quarantine aquarium makes sense only for quarantining newly acquired fish (see p. 34).

Can I catch fish diseases?
Humans can fall prey to the pathogen for fish tuberculosis. Pimplelike wounds that heal slowly or scaly red spots can occur on parts of skin that come into contact with the water. Often they go away by themselves. If they last a fairly long time or increase in size, though, you should certainly consult a skin doctor and explain your hunch. If you have open wounds on your hands, try to avoid putting them into the aquarium.

Can you take a fish to the vet?
Yes, but very few vets specialize in treating fish. So look for a vet before you need one. Many countries have a fish health service; you may be able to get the address from your local university extension service. Some veterinary schools deal in fish diseases and parasitology. You may also find information and addresses on the Internet. You will find some leads on page 60.

What should I do with a fish that is fatally ill?
The simplest method is to use clove oil, which is available in any drugstore. Catch the fish with a net, and put it into a bucket with a couple quarts/liters of water. Add three or four drops per quart/liter of water until the fish goes to sleep. Then raise

A healthy Wagtail Platy always keeps it fins erect.

the dose to 20 drops per quart/liter. You will quickly see by the cessation of gill movement that the fish has gently been put to sleep. Fish from private households can be removed with the trash.

Where can I buy medications for treating fish?

Your pet shop owner may have some relevant training and be able to advise you which medications you can use for specific diseases. Carefully follow the directions on the instruction sheet. If the symptoms are varied, you should never use several medicines at the same time. They may work against each other.

How often must I clean the substrate?

You should clean the whole substrate only when needed, for example when it shows black spots. When you change the water, you can pass the hose closely over the ground, use a finger to stir up the substrate, and suck out the decayed matter. Do the same thing in a different spot every time you change the water, and that way you can put off doing a complete cleaning.

Is a lot of work really part of keeping an aquarium?

In comparison with other house pets, fish do not require a lot of work. You have to check their health and feed them every day plus check the technical devices for proper functioning. The daily time investment averages about 15 minutes. Clean algae off the glass once a week, and trim the plants every two weeks. Depending on how crowded the tank is, every one to two weeks you perform a partial water change. You should also clean the filter every two months.

MY TIPS FOR YOU

Harro Hieronimus

Taking Care of Fish When You Are Away on Vacation

➤ One week before vacation, change the water and check the technical accessories. Make especially sure that the filter is working flawlessly.

➤ For safety while you are away on vacation, install a vibrator pump with an airstone; that way you are on the safe side in case of a defective filter.

➤ Fish up to half the length specified in the portraits can easily live for several days without food. Grown fish can last for two to three weeks without food as long as this does not happen more than twice a year.

➤ If a vacation stand-in takes over feeding, set aside the individual food quantities for each day. Otherwise, the fish are likely to get too much food.

➤ For longer absences and when no one is available to take your place, use an automatic feeder. Test its performance in advance.

Addresses

Associations/Clubs

➤ American Livebearer Association, Timothy Brady, Membership Chairman, 5 Zerby St., Cressonia, PA 17929-1513

➤ Canadian Association of Aquarium Clubs, Miecia Burden, Membership Chair, 142 Stonehenge Place, Kitchener, Ontario, Canada N2N 2M7; 519-745-1452

➤ International Fancy Guppy Association, Paul J. Gorski, Sr., IFGA Treasurer, 2214 Averill Drive, Chesapeake, VA 23323

If you need to find clubs in your area or help with problems (e.g., regulations dealing with fish, help with fish diseases, and so on), these organizations may be able to provide information.

Live-bearers on the Internet

The following Internet pages deal specifically with live-bearing toothcarps. They are a source of advice and contain information on aquarium setup and much more.

➤ www.badmanstropicalfish.com/articles/article 39html (aquatic clubs and associations)

➤ www.tfhmagazine.com/default/aspx?pageid=16 (*Tropical Fish Hobbyist*)

➤ www.bellaonline.com/sitemap/fish (aquarium fish site)

➤ www.xiphophorus.org (Swordtails and Platys)

➤ www.livebearers.org

For questions on the aquarium hobby, consult your local pet shop or Internet chat rooms and bulletin boards.

Books

➤ Dawes, John C. *Livebearing Fishes.* Cassell and Co., 1995

➤ Scott, Peter. *A Fishkeeper's Guide to Livebearing Fishes.* Interpet Publishing, 1999

Magazines

➤ *Aquarium Fish*, 3 Burroughs, Irvine, CA 92618; 949-855-8822

➤ *Tropical Fish Hobbyist*, 1 TFH Plaza, Neptune City, NJ 07753

TO OUR READERS

➤ The electrical devices described in this book for taking care of aquariums must be used with great care.

➤ Keep in mind the dangers involved with electrical appliances and cords, especially in combination with water.

➤ We recommend using a surge protector.

The Author

Harro Hieronimus writes books about aquariums and garden ponds. He is president of the Society for Livebearing Toothcarps and an expert on live-bearing fish.

Photos

Bork: Cover 1, 12, 17 middle, 28, back cover left, right; Giel: 23, 37, 40, 48, 52; Hecker: 34; Hieronimus: 11, 15 left, 17 right, 18, back cover middle; Kahl: inside front cover, 1, 2, 3, 4/5, 7, 8, 14 left, 15 middle, 17 left, 24, 25, 26, 30, 38 left, 39 top left, top right, bottom left, 42, 50, 51, 56, 64; Koenig: 15 right, 16 middle; Linke: 39 bottom right; Peither: 20/21, 29; Reinhard: 16 right, 54; Schmidbauer: 22, 27, 32/33, 36, 38 right, 41, 44, 46/47, 49; Werner: 6, 13, 14 middle, right, 16 left, 35, 43.

All inquiries should be addressed to:
Barron's Educational Series, Inc.
250 Wireless Boulevard
Hauppauge, NY 11788
www.barronseduc.com

Library of Congress Catalog-Card No. 2006043074

ISBN-13: 978-0-7641-3717-4
ISBN-10: 0-7641-3717-4

Library of Congress Cataloging-in-Publication Data
Hieronimus, Harro.
  [Guppy, Platy, Molly und andere Lebendgebärende. English]
  Guppies, mollies, platys, and other live-bearers : purchase, care, feeding, diseases, behavior [and] a special section on breeding / Harro Hieronimus ; drawings by Fritz W. Köhler ; [translated from the German by Eric A. Bye].
    p. cm. — (A complete pet owner's manual)
    Originally published: 1993.
    Includes bibliographical references (p.) and index.
    ISBN-13: 978-0-7641-3717-4
    ISBN-10: 0-7641-3717-4
    1. Livebearing aquarium fishes. I. Title.

SF458.L58H5413 2007
639.3'7667—dc22   2006043074

Printed in China
9 8 7 6 5 4 3 2 1

My Live-bearers

> **Species:** _____

Feeding:

> _____
> _____
> _____

Electrical Devices:

> _____
> _____
> _____

Special Features:

> _____
> _____
> _____

Regular Duties:

> _____
> _____
> _____

Substitute Caregiver When I Am Away on Vacation:

> _____
> _____
> _____

My Pet Shop:

> _____
> _____
> _____

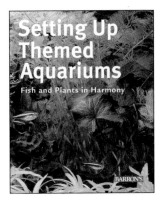
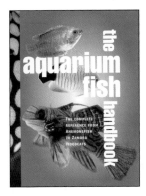
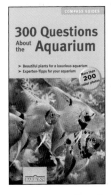

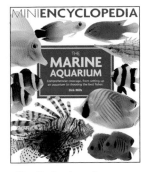
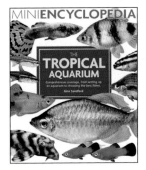

AVOID OVERCROWDING

Since Guppies and similar fish give birth to fully developed young that stand a good **chance of survival** in the presence of thick plantings, the aquarium can quickly become too full. That has a negative impact on **water quality**. So put in only a few fish.

Guaranteed Comfort for Guppies and Their Cohorts

THE RIGHT LOCATION

The aquarium must not get too much sun, because this encourages **algae growth**. Still, it should not be too dark. You can shut off the **lighting** at midday for one or two hours and thus leave it on longer in the evening. That way, working people can get more enjoyment from their fish.

CHANGE WATER FREQUENTLY

Regular water changes are necessary to provide the best possible conditions for the fish. Change **30 percent** of the water at least every two weeks; the fish will thank you with **lively behavior** and bright colors.

THE RIGHT FOOD

Live-bearers have different nutritional needs. Mollies are **algae eaters**, that need lots of plant food. Most other species like variety in their menu because they are omnivores; they can eat dry food with some live and frozen foods.